ARCHITECTURE & DESIGN LIBRARY

EASTERN SPIRIT

ARCHITECTURE & DESIGN LIBRARY

EASTERN SPIRIT

Lisa Jill Schlang

FRIEDMAN/FAIRFAX
PUBLISHERS

A FRIEDMAN/FAIRFAX BOOK

© 2000 by Friedman/Fairfax Publishers

Please visit our website: www.metrobooks.com

Library of Congress Cataloging-in-Publication Data

Schlang, Lisa Jill.
    Eastern spirit / Lisa Jill Schlang.
        p. cm. — (Architecture and design library)
    ISBN 1-58663-025-3 (alk. paper)
        1. Architecture—East Asia.   2. Interior decoration—East Asia.   I. Title.   II. Series.

NA1536 .S35 2000
747.295—dc21

00-037202

Editor: Hallie Einhorn
Art Director: Jeff Batzli
Designer: John Marius
Photography Editor: Erin Feller
Production Managers: Camille Lee and Maria Gonzalez

Color separations by Colourscan Overseas Co Pte Ltd.
Printed in Hong Kong by Midas Printing Limited

1 3 5 7 9 10 8 6 4 2

Distributed by Sterling Publishing Company, Inc.
387 Park Avenue South
New York, NY 10016
Distributed in Canada by Sterling Publishing
c/o Canadian Manda Group
One Atlantic Avenue, Suite 105
Toronto, Ontario, Canada M6K 3E7
Distributed in Australia by
Capricorn Link (Australia) Pty Ltd.
P.O. Box 6651
Baulkham Hills, Business Centre, NSW 2153, Australia

In loving memory of my grandparents, Arthur, Louis, Ruth, and Rosa.

I am especially grateful to all my friends and family for their never-ending enthusiasm and support.
Special thanks to Mom, Dad, Julie, and Eric.

Contents

INTRODUCTION

Architecture and interior design, like fashion, are substantially influenced by the world around them. And thanks to the Internet, television, and technological advances in transportation, the world has gradually become a much smaller place. With the resulting cross-fertilization of cultures, it is no surprise that today's homes are more eclectic than ever before. And one aesthetic that we've come to embrace readily is that of the Far East. While certain aspects of Asian design have experienced renewed popularity over the last few years, Westerners have been fascinated by this region and its offerings for centuries. Unlike the way in which we eagerly follow and then just as quickly tire of most trends, we can't seem to get enough of design elements that have their origins in the Far East, particularly China and Japan.

Steeped in tradition, symbolism, and spirituality, Chinese and Japanese design elements offer an exoticism like no other. The minimalism of Japanese-style interiors refreshes and soothes the soul in an inexplicable way, and the warmth of finely crafted Chinese pieces imbues the rooms they adorn with subtle elegance. Whether it's the colors, textures, forms, or mystical qualities that stir our emotions, Eastern style seems to resonate with a great many of us.

To what do we attribute the enduring enthusiasm toward Japanese and Chinese design? Perhaps it stems from the long history of these ancient cultures, which have produced a mélange of motifs, ranging from beautifully detailed traditional furnishings featuring intricate carvings and hand-painted designs to contemporary monochromatic spaces and streamlined forms. Although Asian decorative arts and architecture can be traced back to the Neolithic Age (c. 9000–6000 B.C.E.), both old and new examples of construction, furnishings, and decorative accents have been influenced by one predominant factor: religion.

While the landscapes and governments of Eastern countries have developed and evolved over the years, the peoples' dedication to spirituality has remained constant. The various religions and philosophies

OPPOSITE: *Chinese scroll paintings are an elegant means for adding an Eastern flair to an interior. The ones shown here feature calligraphy, an art form that dates back to the Shang dynasty (c. 1766–1122 B.C.E.). In general, the quality of such work is dependent upon the pressure applied while creating the brush strokes. Scroll paintings are often given as gifts.*

in Asia offer different theories, each of which has contributed to how people live. For example, Confucianism, founded by the Chinese philosopher Confucius (c. 551–479 B.C.E.), promoted a set of ethical precepts and sought to achieve order; from Confucianism came architectural forms that were rigid and symmetrical. Taoism, also originating in China, complemented Confucianism with its concept of balancing forces, known as yin and yang. In addition, Taoism and the Japanese Shintoism are responsible for the ecological sensibility that has guided many Asian builders and architects.

Of all the Eastern religions and philosophies, Zen Buddhism has had the strongest impact on design. Embracing theories similar to those of Taoism, striving for harmony in the universe, Buddhism arose in India during the sixth century B.C.E. The sect known by the Japanese name Zen and the Chinese name Chan began in 520 C.E. when Bodhidharma, a Chinese monk, brought Buddhism to China from India. Having flourished in China during the Tang dynasty (c.618–907 C.E.), the religion made its way into Japan five hundred years later. Based on self-discipline through meditation, Zen dictates a life of simplicity. The goal is to attain a state of spiritual enlightenment, referred to as satori, which can be reached only through the elimination of superfluous elements in one's life. Thus, the materials used to create a Zen-like effect are pure, simple, and ideally, natural. In ancient times, houses were often made of a wood skeleton set in a pillar-and-beam construction said to signify the tree under which the Buddha found enlightenment. This type of framework has been employed in many Eastern structures ever since.

From a practical standpoint, many Asian residences have been and continue to be made of wood because of this material's strength and availability. Similarly, stone is common in Japanese and Chinese residences. Symbolic of permanence, it offers a combination of sensuality and durability that has appealed to Easterners for centuries. Today, many features once made of stone are constructed of concrete,

which can be honed for a smooth finish similar to marble or granite or left rough to resemble heavily textured rock. The material's versatility allows for many design options: it can be infused with colors and cast or poured to create floors, walls, and countertops. Rooms and structures that include concrete afford a cool, tranquil Zen-like ambience.

While the materials bring an innate beauty to Asian forms, designs frequently reflect a specific belief or symbolic idea. The Chinese, for example, believe that the universe is made up of five elements—wood, fire, earth, metal, and water. Also known as "phases," these elements are embedded in Chinese cosmology, an astrophysical study of the dynamics of the universe, which dates back to the Shang dynasty (c. 1766–1122 B.C.E.). These elements are represented by five animals—the sheep, hen, ox, dog, and pig, respectively—or five tigers. And each element and animal has special meaning and symbolism. Both the tiger and the ox, for example, represent strength. The belief in their mystical qualities has caused many of these basic natural elements and creatures to make their way into the home. For instance, tigers appear on scroll paintings that adorn walls, and water flows through fountains. Wood, which can appear in all sorts of forms in a residence, is associated with wealth and family.

The five elements form the basis of the eight trigrams that are used in feng shui—the Chinese art of placement—to assess the qualities of a

OPPOSITE: *Many elements of Asian design stem from Zen Buddhism. Here, a typical place of worship, housed in a skeleton of wood, has a statue of Buddha as its central focus. Sitting in the lotus position, the figure demonstrates the gesture Bhumisparsha-mura, or "touching the earth." One hand is placed upon the lap, and the other on the knee. According to legend, this was the position of Shakyamuni, the founder of Buddhism, at the moment of his enlightenment.*

ABOVE: *Earthy textures and hues often have a soothing effect. Here, a mushroom-hued ottoman, a small candle, and a black clay bowl holding a floating flower form a peaceful vignette. Southern Asia is home to numerous aquatic plants, including the lotus, which has great symbolism. It is the Chinese emblem of summer, and in Buddhism, it represents the essence of human nature.*

OPPOSITE: *A room can adopt the principles of Zen design without manifesting a particularly Asian tone. This bedroom exudes a sense of calm, thanks to the incorporation of natural materials, a minimal use of furnishings, and a wall of windows that invites the garden beyond into the space. The pale neutral palette further contributes to the restful ambience.*

structure. Tellingly, the phrase feng shui means "wind and water." Adapted from the Taoist principles of yin and yang, the practice centers on creating harmony. According to the philosophy, achieving this balance will lead to happiness in different areas of life.

Unlike Zen, feng shui does not promote minimalism. Rather, it focuses on creating a positive flow of energy, called *ch'i*. Consideration is given to the relationships between spaces. And certain arrangements, such as the strategic placement of wind chimes and mirrors, help to combat negative energy. Materials and colors also come into play. To reach the perfect balance, there needs to be an equilibrium of hard and soft, smooth and reflective surfaces. For example, when it comes to flooring, one might mix a hard yang material such as marble, which speeds up the flow of ch'i, with a soft yin material such as sisal, which slows down ch'i.

The feng shui phenomenon and the tremendous popularity of Zen interiors have proved that Eastern design has longevity. And indeed, Westerners have been borrowing from and adapting Asian styles for years. During the past century alone, Asian design principles have appeared in the works of Arts and Crafts pioneers and modernists. World-renowned architect Frank Lloyd Wright, for example, looked to the East for much inspiration. Interpretations of Asian design elements and philosophies can be seen in many of his creations, including his masterpiece Fallingwater, with its cantilevered slabs set over a waterfall—a seamless integration of site and architecture.

Thanks to the adaptability of Eastern design, bringing an Eastern flavor to a home can be relatively simple. There is no need for a total remodeling or makeover. In most cases, a few strong pieces, a couple of basic design principles, or even a single evocative architectural detail may be all you need to conjure images of the Far East.

CHAPTER ONE

EASTERN EXTERIORS

When it comes to creating a structure that provides shelter, Eastern designers are very practical. And it is a combination of this practicality, myriad spiritual and philosophical beliefs, and fine craftsmanship that has guided the architecture of Eastern homes. When studying traditional structures of the Far East, one sees how both site and climate play large roles in the design sensibility.

Understanding the Asian landscape facilitates an understanding of the building limitations. The island country of Japan, for instance, includes both highlands and lowlands, rural and urban areas. And the complex topography of China, the most heavily populated country in the world, consists of steep hillsides, plains that run down to great river systems, narrow river valleys, desert basins, and high plateaus. This tremendous geographic diversity has had a direct effect on the climate and on how houses are built. So, throughout Asia, houses range from subterranean structures to ones set high on mountaintops. Each area demands its own set of materials and guidelines.

In most parts of the Far East, heavy rainfalls, high humidity, and earthquakes dictate architectural design decisions. By examining the evolution of Asian dwellings, one can trace the learning curve of builders dealing with harsh conditions. Few Chinese structures predating the Ming dynasty (c. 1368–1644 C.E.) exist today since most were destroyed by natural disasters or wars. What we know about the early houses in Japan is that they were formed by erecting two poles that were then joined by a ridgepole. Logs placed at an angle became the walls of the home and interlocked at the top, creating an almost tentlike structure. Later, the configuration of the walls took on a boxlike shape, while the interlocking logs were used only for the roof. It is this form that is the basis for the modern-day houses.

Many Asian structures are made of wood and have a pillar-and-beam construction. In China, this framing system is referred to as *tailiang*. The Chinese also employ a pillars-and-traverse tie beam

OPPOSITE: *Inspiration from Eastern design can yield pleasing results. Here, the Asian influence is apparent in the use of wood, the geometry of forms, the overhanging roof, and the abundance of windows. The striking picture window, located front and center, not only fills the house with natural light, but also helps to usher in the outdoors.*

framework, called *chuandou*. During ancient times in both China and Japan, the wood shell had a mud floor beneath it. But Easterners quickly realized that they needed to create a foundation so that the wood beams would not rot from heavy rainfalls. The Chinese employed stone foundations, and the Japanese followed suit. The stone was often laid beyond the length of the structure to provide added protection from moisture. In modern times, concrete has come to replace stone.

Much thought has been given to the roofs of Eastern houses over the years. Because of heavy rains, many roofs slope, allowing water to drain off the sides. The steepness of the roof is determined by the amount of rainfall. The heavier the rain, the more severe the slope. Only in arid areas is a flat roof employed.

Roof styles are many and varied. Humble dwellings feature simple roofs with straight lines, while homes in affluent areas display graceful curves and sweeping profiles. Overhanging eaves provide protection from the rain and sun. In humid areas, roofs are made of water-repellent materials, such as rice straw and wild grasses. Tiles are also employed because they are quite impervious to the elements. A bonding layer of mud provides stability for the tiles, but occasionally after a harsh storm, they need to be reset. Convex tiles form gutters to further protect the structure beneath from rain. Other materials used for roofs include bark, slate, clay, and bamboo.

Architects and designers also have to consider ventilation strategies and ways of shading interiors from the sun, especially in warm, humid climates. Latticework is a sensible and common means for dividing areas, as it allows air to flow freely between spaces. Covered walkways, designed to provide shelter from the rain and sun, are also often found in the Far East. Many Chinese homes include courtyards that link one building to another. Within the courtyards, one generally finds paths, fountains, and some greenery, though these areas do not take the form of actual gardens. In China, very few private gardens exist, but Imperial parks and scholar gardens offer inspiration and beauty.

In the Far East, gardens and courtyards, considered "outdoor rooms," establish natural transitions from interior spaces to the surrounding landscape and outside world. The traditional Japanese garden takes into account scale and proportion. With these factors in mind, plants, trees, moss, rocks, and sand are all carefully situated. Much attention is given to color as well. For instance, a garden may be planted with only red flowers.

Working in tandem with the plants, pathways meander through many Japanese gardens, presenting residents and visitors with surprises at every turn. Those walking through the garden get a glimpse of what is to come through strategically placed trees or shrubs.

In contrast to gardens featuring lush greenery and blooms, Zen gardens usually consist of dry rock or gravel. The design is an exercise in control, reinforcing the Zen philosophy that there should be no superfluous elements to distract onlookers from finding enlightenment.

OPPOSITE: *A cool reflection of this Ming dynasty–style structure can be seen through the weeping branches of a nearby tree. Set in the Huangshan area of China, the building features a stone walkway, an arched entry, and walls designed to be impervious to the surrounding water. Red paint adds a vibrant touch to the otherwise subdued scene.*

LEFT: *A bamboo fence made up of vertical and horizontal forms lends a rustic quality to the otherwise formal Himeji Castle in Japan. The grand multileveled structure features an elegant roofline with a series of brackets. The prevalence of stone imparts a sense of strength and solidity.*

ABOVE: *In ancient Japan, tile roofs were reserved for temples and castles and were indicative of high social status. But during the past two to three centuries, the Japanese extended the use of tile roofs to homes in general so as to provide them with the necessary protection. Here, green tiles in various tones pick up the color of the trees above. The undulating forms allow water to drain off the structure during heavy rainfalls.*

OPPOSITE: *Located in the mountain village of Ogamachi, Japan, this house is built in the* gassho-zukuri *style. Gassho-zukuri, which translates as "praying hands," is an early building method that employs two poles and a joining ridgepole to create a steep rafter offering shelter. The shape of the resulting form led to the name.*

ABOVE: *A stone pathway leads spectators through a verdant temple garden. In Eastern gardens, the placement of each stone is carefully calculated, and such factors as shape, size, and color all come into play. The absence of flowering plants is deliberate, as Zen practitioners believe that colorful flowers are frivolous. Instead, followers of Zen incorporate evergreen trees, which are thought to be symbolic of eternity.*

LEFT: *Set atop a stone foundation, a stately pillar provides support. Red painted latticework displays an airiness that lightens the pillar's massive quality. Notice how the doors and the brackets underneath the roof are also painted red. According to ancient mystical beliefs, this hue wards off evil spirits and brings good luck.*

ABOVE: *Zen gardens traditionally demonstrate restraint and are therefore limited in materials. In this fastidious Zen garden, manicured shrubbery and raked sand are the primary elements. The clean lines and forms afford a feeling of tranquillity.*

LEFT: *Thanks to a covered walkway with rounded wooden supports, residents and guests can enjoy the courtyard during inclement weather. Typical of the Japanese home, the simple geometric detailing found in the architecture is what provides visual interest, not elaborate ornamentation.*

ABOVE: *Reminiscent of the latticework from Japanese houses in the* shoin *style, the back of this bench presents a grid formation. The seating, made of bamboo stalks, allows visitors to enjoy the low plantings and gravel ground cover. And what better place for a serene Eastern garden than amid the urban bustle?*

LEFT: *Natural materials make up this Zen Buddhist retreat, allowing it to blend in with the surrounding landscape. Located in Carmel Valley, California, the structure consists of various geometric forms that create a sense of balance and overall harmony. The stone edging of the pond and walkway enhances the natural look of the setting.*

ABOVE: *This modern structure emulates Japanese design in its blurring of the boundaries between indoors and out. The effect is accomplished by vast expanses of glass, which reveal a Zen-inspired decor that includes bare walls and little in the way of furniture or decorative objects. The architecture itself exhibits a Zen-like quality with its clean, straightforward lines.*

ABOVE: *Underneath a wooden roof sheltering a porch, a pagoda-style lantern hangs to provide illumination outdoors. Below, a Japanese garden filled with large stones and bamboo posts beckons visitors. It's hard to believe this Eastern-style vignette is set in London, England.*

RIGHT: *Bridges are fundamental elements of Asian gardens. Here, an unpainted wooden bridge over a stream provides passage to and from the house. To maintain simplicity, bridges are often left with a natural wood finish. Those that are not set over water usually act as devices to promote meditation.*

ABOVE: *This ornamental bridge is both decorative and functional. The gradual curve of the arch manifests a fluid quality that echoes the water beneath it, while the red hue complements the surrounding greenery.*

OPPOSITE: *This pavilion in San Francisco's Golden Gate Park lends a foreign flair to the California landscape. Set beneath a palm tree, the structure provides a shady resting spot for passersby drawn to the Eastern sensibility.*

ABOVE: *Illustrating the desire to integrate indoors and out, this dwelling opens onto a refreshing garden setting. The enticing scene includes plenty of greenery, a stone path, and a demure bridge. A wood fence with a stepped design encloses the outdoor space.*

ABOVE: *Central courtyards often link traditional family compounds in China. The outdoor space provides a place for gathering, sharing meals, and delving into private contemplation. Here, two typical Eastern structures—one painted red with upturned eaves and the other with impressive black doors sporting gold detailing—are joined by a courtyard that features an arbor of greenery. Notice that the gilded designs on the doors form circular patterns. In many Eastern cultures, the circle is symbolic of eternity, as there is no beginning and no end to its form.*

ABOVE: *While raked gravel makes up most of this courtyard, large rocks, greenery, and brightly colored plants have been incorporated to provide additional visual interest. The mélange of colors, shapes, and textures softens the hard edges of the surrounding structure and creates an inviting atmosphere. Chairs situated under the shelter of a covered walkway provide a prime spot for quiet reflection.*

A B O V E : *This pavilion in Kyoto, Japan, is enhanced by the outdoor greenery. The shape of the building mimics nature, as its sheltering eaves and vertical timbers repeat the lines of the surrounding trees.*

CHAPTER TWO

SHAPING SPACE AND LIGHT

Visions of open minimalist spaces divided only by screens, or rooms filled with just the right balance of finely crafted antiques, are what come to mind when thinking of Eastern-style interiors. The distinct designs that emanate from the Far East are unique to the cultures there. Most revolve around a desire to bring elements of nature indoors, a deft use of light and space, and a careful selection of color and materials.

The inclusion of nature is apparent in all types of Asian homes. Incorporating the outdoors into one's living space establishes a natural harmony and reinforces the balance of yin and yang. Natural materials, such as wood and stone, are the building blocks of most residences. Whenever possible, these materials are left exposed to glorify their inherent beauty. An abundance of windows and doors provides easy access to the outdoors, and homes are frequently designed with terraces and verandas. In China, especially in the Beijing area, many residences open onto a courtyard. But the veneration of nature is not limited to architectural features alone. Furnishings may boast lavishly painted flowers or landscapes, and in many homes, small gardens set indoors literally bring nature inside.

Eastern design treats space as a blank canvas from which to work. Most residences are based on a rigid geometry. While the concept of one-room living may have arisen out of economic limitations, it still exists today. Most Japanese houses are in the shoin style and consist of a single room that is merely partitioned off. Many Chinese houses, on the other hand, have rooms that appear to radiate out from a central axis perpendicularly.

In Japanese homes, the form that the interior space takes is shaped by where the pillars and beams are placed, and the size is referred to by the number of tatami mats that line the floor. Measuring about three feet (.9m) by six feet (1.8m), tatami mats are constructed of straw and a supportive backing. Even today, real estate agents will

OPPOSITE: *The definition of separate areas is an important aspect of Japanese design. This sitting area is sectioned off from the adjacent bedroom by sliding screen doors. Muted tones of gray and brown create a subdued setting with a restful quality—perfect for an area intended for sleep and relaxation.*

ornamentation in the Japanese home, the tokonoma often features a beautiful hand-painted scroll or an exquisite flower arrangement.

But partitions and physical forms are not the only factors that determine the look of an interior. Light plays an integral role as well. In fact, it is the interplay of light and shade that controls the ambience of the setting. Throughout the day, as the light changes, so will the atmosphere. In China, the orientation of the structure is carefully planned to make the most of natural light, while the inclusion of latticework results in wonderful patterns on floors. In Japan, translucent screens diffuse natural light entering the interior. Paper lanterns provide artificial light when necessary.

Light also affects color. In monochromatic schemes, for example, visual interest comes from the relationship between light and shadow. Rich materials and textures contribute appeal as well. Delicate paper screens meet hardwood floors with graceful graining running through them, and rounded lanterns provide contrast with the graphic grid of the shoji. The result is a calming environment in which the various elements work together.

describe a space as being, say, a twelve-mat room. The interior is then divided by either shoji or *fusuma* screens. The former are constructed of translucent paper and cedar latticework. Lightweight, shoji screens are generally set on a very small track so they can slide back and forth easily. The fusuma screens are made with an opaque fabric.

Changes in levels and the shapes of spaces are also important. For example, in northern Chinese houses, a raised brick platform called a *kang* distributes heat from the cooking area to adjacent bedrooms in the winter. And in Japan, alcoves are created to showcase decorative objects. This type of alcove, called a *tokonoma*, typically contains a few shelves and is part of a sitting area. Being the only place for

LEFT: *At the heart of Zen design lies a purity of form. This sensual composition owes its appeal to an eloquent pairing of natural textures and simple, unassuming lines.*

OPPOSITE: *Natural wood tones enhance this minimalist setting. Additional color comes from the vase, which serves as a link to the greenery of the landscape beyond.*

OPPOSITE: *A sliding shoji screen is left open to encourage enjoyment of the rock garden beyond. A sole wooden bench, the simplicity of which is in keeping with the space's mood, invites occupants to contemplate nature. During inclement weather, the room can be securely closed off by the translucent doors, which nonetheless maintain the airy ambience.*

ABOVE: *A low-slung, clean-lined table and a shoji screen with black framing are warmed by a pair of candles and a golden cushion. The setting has a sanctuary-like quality and is perfect for meditation or reading.*

RIGHT: *Flourishing in the humid climate, orchids are readily available in the East. Here, they team up with a small lantern to form an enchanting vignette that exudes an Eastern sensibility. A simple grouping such as this can easily be incorporated into any home to celebrate the beauty of nature.*

ABOVE: *Minimalism is essential in designing a setting that adheres to the principles of Zen Buddhism. Spaces need to be free of distractions that might get in the way of finding enlightenment. Despite the spareness of this space, it projects a certain warmth, thanks to the combination of textures, the subtle variations of soothing neutral tones, and the soft natural light entering through the translucent screens.*

OPPOSITE: *Western architects have long been intrigued by the unpretentiousness of Japanese design. In a living room belonging to and created by modernist Charles Eames, a wall of glass brings the outside in and pays homage to the Japanese shoji screen. The openness of the space completes the effect.*

ABOVE: *Thanks to the minimalist aesthetic of this Japanese tea ceremony room, the few architectural elements and accents that are present have a powerful impact. The curved ceiling acts as a foil for the straight lines and right angles of the tokonoma, which houses a scroll painting and a decorative vase. The tokonoma serves as a focal point that aids contemplation.*

ABOVE: *The importance of a Japanese tea ceremony room is highlighted by its location on a separate raised level. Here, sliding screen doors close when privacy is desired, while two contemporary chairs provide contrast to the traditional-style atmosphere. The result is a sophisticated setting with an exotic flavor.*

ABOVE: *Flanking a doorway, two Chinese cupboards that feature traditional hardware create a picture of symmetry and foster a sense of equilibrium. The Chinese scroll painting centered beyond draws the eye through the passage. Meanwhile, golden walls present a luminous backdrop that flatters the dark wood pieces.*

ABOVE: *At the top of a staircase, a striking reddish-brown wall announces the entrance to a second-story living area and offsets the pale tones beyond. The black wooden table mimics the lines of a traditional Chinese altar table, which would be found in the reception area of a home. Such tables were originally designed as a place for guests to leave offerings—often vases or bowls for incense.*

LEFT: *It's difficult to tell where the room ends and the outdoor area begins, thanks to smooth expanses of glass uninterrupted by mullions or leading. The earthy hues and textures of the matting and bamboo shades heighten the connection with the outdoors, further obscuring any notion of boundaries. Other natural textures abound, from the rocks and leafy plant to the wooden floor and chest.*

BELOW: *Rounded stones provide an earthy counterpoint to the sleek surfaces of this peaceful bath. Edging the tub, the smooth pebbles create the sensation of bathing in a lake. Notice how their coloring echoes that of the tub and the lower portion of the wall.*

ABOVE: *When all the tones of a setting, particularly a garden, are neutral, it is important to pay close attention to texture for diversity. Here, smooth pieces of cherry wood and a rough sisal mat pair up with an interior Japanese rock garden, which includes both rough and smooth stones. In Asian cultures, the rock signifies permanence and stability. Demonstrating a balance of colors, textures, and proportions, the carefully designed grouping conveys a feeling of harmony.*

ABOVE: *Hand-painted furnishings are popular in China and Japan, and flowers are a common motif, as they represent spring and beauty. In fact, Japan's national emblem is the cherry tree.*

ABOVE: *This serene space is designed not for spiritual endeavors, but for storage. Richly hued wooden cabinetry keeps audio-visual materials hidden away and prevents clutter from disrupting the rest of the home. Thanks to the symmetrical configuration of the cabinets, the space conveys a reassuring sense of order.*

ABOVE: *Bamboo reeds form a tactile wall that brings nature indoors. In the middle of the highly textural expanse, wooden planks feature markings that appear to be abstract representations of birds. In many Eastern cultures, the bird is symbolic of the soul and is often thought of as the embodiment of air. The legs of the coffee table resemble the inwardly curving ones of Chinese kang-style pieces.*

ABOVE: *This living room demonstrates an Eastern sensibility in its emphasis on the natural landscape. A soaring wall of glass makes the grass, trees, and lake part of the decor, while sliding glass doors encourage residents to spend time outside. Additional Asian influences can be seen in the low-slung table and the use of both wood and stone.*

ABOVE: *Asian design embraced the concept of the "great room" long before Westerners did. Many Eastern homes feature large open spaces that serve multiple functions and provide access to the outdoors so that the family can be closer to nature. This capacious room includes wood floors, a decorative kimono, and seating mats around a sunken hearth.*

ABOVE: *A mixture of light sources—both natural and artificial—is responsible for the allure of this garden, which brings the natural world inside. Sunlight enters from above and reflects off the rocks below; a lantern highlights greenery in the corner; and fixtures in the adjacent space beyond the screen cast a warm glow. In the center of the scene rests a stone water trough.*

CHAPTER THREE
GATHERING AREAS

More and more, Western homes are being designed with one expansive open room that serves a number of functions. Generally, this space takes the form of a great room and includes a dining area, living room, and kitchen. Eastern design has long embraced this type of gathering space, and many traditional Asian dwellings feature a large room that contains separate areas for clearly defined purposes. Other public spaces of importance in Eastern homes include outdoor rooms and transitional settings. For example, the *genkan*, which is the Japanese entry hall, provides a place to leave one's shoes before walking into the main part of the home. Those entering then approach a raised wooden platform where slippers are worn.

In Eastern design, there is a distinction between a home's public spaces, which are designed for entertaining, and the private ones, which are geared toward family. As is the case in many of today's Western dwellings, the kitchen is the center of the home. It not only serves as a place for meal preparation, but accommodates various casual activities as well. In contrast to North American homes, though, there is not much furniture. Because possessions are considered burdens, Zen-inspired kitchens have only the bare essentials, and necessary items are neatly stored away when not in use. As a result, these rooms seem spacious and bear an open, airy quality.

In terms of the five elements, the kitchen is where fire is housed. Because of its ability to turn solids into liquids, fire is the element that signifies transformation. In China, fire is positive and considered yang. And in early Buddhist art, Shakyamuni, the founder of Buddhism, is represented as a flaming pillar.

Thoughts of Eastern-style dining spaces evoke images of beautiful tableware. Cool hues, seen in celadon ceramics and black lacquerware, dominate. These colors combine with carefully chosen forms,

OPPOSITE: *Creating a Zen-like setting requires discipline. Here, the pieces are few but deliberate. A tightly woven rug, barely visible atop the light wood floor, and a white screen establish a quiet backdrop for a sculptural chair and a dark-hued runner. Yellow tulips in a frosted glass vase add a whisper of color and provide a softening effect.*

such as square-shaped dishes and perfectly rounded bowls, to create graceful vessels for serving food.

The history of Asian tableware is extensive. Glazed ceramics, for instance, were first seen during the Chou dynasty (c. 1122–256 B.C.E.) in China. The production of ceramics achieved great heights during the Ming dynasty (c. 1368–1644 C.E.), which also saw the introduction of an enameling process involving a new double-firing technique that allowed a variety of colors to be applied to porcelain. Chopsticks, perhaps the items that first come to mind in association with Eastern-style dining, also originated in China. Made of ivory, wood, or bamboo, these utensils were adopted in almost all the surrounding countries.

The simple, streamlined elegance of Asian tableware has inspired many Western designers. Indeed, manufacturers of home furnishings and accessories now produce a variety of dishes, bowls, cups, teapots, and serving pieces in Eastern-style designs. Another dining-related element that has been borrowed by Westerners is the low-slung table. In Japan, dining takes place while seated on the floor, so the tables are naturally lower. While Westerners generally do not take their meals in this manner, the aesthetic of these pieces has had tremendous appeal. Some homeowners pair up such tables with low banquettes for comfortable relaxed dining.

The serving and drinking of tea plays an important role in Asian cultures. The Japanese tea ceremony as it is known today originated in the sixteenth century, but lavish tea parties existed even earlier. The typical ceremony requires a special alcove area where the host can serve tea to guests. Adhering to the principles of Zen Buddhism, the space needs to be orderly. It is carefully planned to create a balance of yin and yang. The alcove is usually designed with a series of shelves to store the various serving pieces. Adapting ideas from the Japanese tea room will lend an elegant simplicity to any space.

ABOVE: *A typical Japanese teahouse has a very low entry with an upwardly sloping ceiling and a main area with two other distinct ceiling designs, each made of different materials. Here, however, we see a modern interpretation enlisting only a couple of traditional features, including tatami mats on the floor and an alcove fitted with shelves.*

OPPOSITE: *You can create an uncluttered look in the kitchen by hiding everyday necessities, such as cookbooks, place mats, and dishware, behind sliding doors. Here, deep storage shelves are camouflaged by paper-and-wood screens set on tracks.*

ABOVE: *The interplay of rectangular forms, which rise from the floor to the cabinetry to the screens, takes these simple shapes from ordinary to extraordinary. The gray tile floor, the abundance of glass, and the sleekness of the counter contribute to the tranquillity of the space.*

ABOVE: *Dressed in white and accented by wood and black detailing, this space has an aura of calmness about it. Streamlined forms and balanced proportions further contribute to the Zen-like ambience. A bar area, which is built slightly higher than the work surface of the island, serves as a convenient spot for breakfast and snacks. It also hides any mess on the lower counter, thereby maintaining the appearance that everything is under control.*

OPPOSITE: *Graced with views of the sky and trees, this living-dining space features wood floors, sliding glass doors, and a concrete hearth. A mat strategically situated to make the most of the outdoor scenery and fresh air provides an enticing spot for tea. The space just goes to show that an Eastern aesthetic can form the basis of a stylish decor in any home.*

ABOVE: *In Eastern cultures, the tableware is chosen to complement the food. Here, vegetables and chopsticks have been artfully arranged on stacked square plates, creating an almost sculptural effect.*

ABOVE: *Sliding panels extend this room to the Japanese garden beyond, while bamboo blinds and an overhang shade the interior to keep it cool. Tatami mats offer comfort underfoot, and pillows provide seating at the low table. An elegant scroll painting hangs on display in the tokonoma.*

ABOVE: *Zen-like in their display, four chairs, four bowls, and four spoons create a feeling of peace. White lilies echo the hue of the bowls, while a red wall provides a flattering backdrop that is vivid but not jarring. All the components come together to form a scene that is simple yet striking.*

OPPOSITE: *A traditionally decorated dining area with a dark wood table gets a touch of exoticism from the addition of grass-cloth wall coverings, an Oriental chest, and a Japanese-style hanging lamp. Sliding glass doors open the space to the landscape and make the room seem larger.*

RIGHT: *A close-up of the chest in the dining room reveals the rich texture of the wood. Notice how the curving lines of the intricate hardware echo the swirls of the graining.*

OPPOSITE: *In some cases, mixing a variety of styles can be a disaster. Here, however, the attempt is a complete success. In the background, an antique Asian chest mingles comfortably with a mid-twentieth-century Eames lounge chair and a contemporary lamp. Thanks to a wide doorway, these elements are on display for occupants of the dining area, where an Eastern-style painted screen bearing strong gold tones serves as a refreshing counterpoint to a straightforward dark wood table. Along with a glass and chrome light fixture and a pair of silver candlesticks, these features create an inviting setting.*

ABOVE: *A yin and yang effect is achieved in this dining space: the cool whites of the walls, window treatment, dishes, and lamp shade counterbalance the deep reddish-brown hues of the side table, dining table, and planter. The resulting picture is one of perfect harmony.*

OPPOSITE: *Sectioning off the space from the rest of the home, a Japanese paper screen provides a soothing backdrop in this dining room. Keeping the furnishings to a minimum and juxtaposing light and dark elements are design strategies that create a dramatic effect.*

RIGHT: *The decor of this contemporary living room is based on ancient Asian design elements. The focal point of the space is a modern sofa in a bold red hue that immediately attracts attention. Ceramics and pillows are decorated with calligraphy, an art of lettering that has been practiced for centuries in the Far East. Japanese-style lanterns and shojilike screens ensure plenty of light. Even the rug is reminiscent of the natural fiber used for tatami mats.*

ABOVE: *In this eclectic living room, the various furnishings, including such Asian-style elements as a folding screen and a small table with an upturned top, are tied together by their neutral hues. Subtle touches of color—an orange toss pillow, blue-gray upholstery on the chaise, and cheery yellow flowers—make the space seem welcoming without disrupting the serene mood. The screen not only tempers the amount of sunlight that penetrates the room, but, juxtaposed against the tall windows, brings a more intimate scale to the space as well.*

ABOVE: *Infusing a room with an Eastern tone often requires just a few key pieces. In this comfortable living room, all it takes is a delicate orchid, a folding screen, and a refined scroll painting.*

ABOVE: *Together, these pieces from the Far East form an interesting mix. The linear arrangement of the Chinese splat-back chair, the chest, and the table calls attention to their staggered heights. A scroll featuring a tiger brings to mind the Chinese concept of the five elements, represented by five tigers.*

ABOVE: *Two Chinese cabinets anchor this symmetrically arranged living room. But the placement of these furnishings is not the only element that brings a sense of equilibrium to the space's eclectic mix. Complementary hues—green and red—counterbalance each other and contribute to the harmony of the setting.*

CHAPTER FOUR
RELAXING RETREATS

The bedroom is the one place where we can find a moment of privacy. It is a retreat shut off from the rest of the world, and it is the place where dreams are literally made. Since the room's primary purpose is to foster relaxation, it is important that there be a balance between yin and yang. Harmony in the bedroom will help lead to a peaceful night's rest.

Toward that end, the bedroom in a Zen-like setting includes plenty of storage so that all superfluous items are hidden out of sight. In rooms that follow the art and science of feng shui, the relationship of the bed to the entrance is of great importance. To promote ch'i, the bed should be placed on a diagonal from the door. And to enhance romance and passion, one should place something purple on the south side of the bedroom.

The most distinctive feature of a Japanese bedroom is the futon. A thick quilt that can be folded up during the day to increase living space, this device offers versatility and maintains a state of simplicity. When in use, the futon lies atop the thin tatami mats that line bedroom floors. Made of natural grasses, these mats offer texture in otherwise unadorned spaces. The absence of fussy embellishment instills a sense of serenity and allows the architecture, as well as the few select pieces of furniture, to take on profound significance.

But a bedroom does not need a futon or tatami mats to convey an Eastern mood. With its clean, unpretentious lines, a platform bed can take the place of a futon and still maintain an Eastern look. Pairing such a bed with a shoji-style screen will not only heighten the Eastern tone, but also brighten up a bedroom that doesn't receive much natural light. In more heavily furnished retreats, bamboo blinds, a generous use of other natural materials, and a couple of specifically Asian pieces, such as a Chinese marriage chest (which can be used to store

OPPOSITE: *Built-in storage flanking a wooden bed allows all extraneous elements to be concealed, creating an environment free of distraction. On the closet doors, paperlike panels featuring bamboo designs heighten the natural look and Asian tone of the room. The only decorative accents are an orchid and a small collection of celadon cups, both of which are in keeping with the mood.*

linens) or a painted folding screen (which can be used to section off storage space) will inject an Eastern flavor.

When it comes to the bath, a minimalist aesthetic tends to prevail. As a cleansing ritual for body and spirit alike, bathing has been taken very seriously in Asian design. In the traditional Japanese ritual, bathers first take a shower or wash themselves using a bucket of water to get rid of any impurities before stepping into the bath. After they have cleansed themselves, they can enjoy a meditative soak. Soaking tubs, made from cypress, cedar, teak, stone, or concrete, are deeper than Western-style baths so that the water easily covers the bather's shoulders. Although today there are not as many soaking tubs as in the past, the layout of the typical Japanese home still consists of a separate shower and tub.

The Japanese view bathing as a form of relaxation and rejuvenation. As a result, the baths display a refined elegance. The use of natural materials, such as wood for floors or bamboo for walls, brings harmony to the space. Clean lines and pared-down forms will also promote a Zen-like atmosphere. When all these elements are combined, the result is a room that offers the ultimate in tranquillity.

ABOVE: *This contemporary bath takes its inspiration from Japanese styling. The shape of the tub is reminiscent of the traditional soaking tub, and the shower, though close by, is separate. Cream-colored tiles are used for both amenities to achieve a seamless look.*

OPPOSITE: *Dressed in white linens, a futon is the focal point of this bedroom. At first glance, the decor seems very basic, but on closer examination, we see that the room is filled with details: a bamboo shade, wood flooring, wood-and-paper doors, and an array of artwork, all of which combine to ensure a sense of harmony.*

ABOVE: *Sliding glass doors bring the occupants of this bedroom closer to nature. A low table, a futon, and a small chest provide all the functional furnishings needed.*

ABOVE: *Carefully chosen furnishings and natural materials infuse this bedroom with an Eastern spirit. The wood enclosed bed makes for a peaceful retreat, while a series of shelves within the structure allows homeowners to keep their favorite treasures close at hand. A Chinese altar table supports other collectibles on display.*

ABOVE: *This bedroom takes its cues from Eastern design, as demonstrated by the simplicity of the neutral palette and the powerful symmetry of the bed. The sense of balance comes from not only the arrangement of the bed pillows, but also the placement of the fabric panels on the headboard. With their proportions and vertical orientation, these panels present a scroll-like appearance. The hues of the bed linens, the chrome and glass night table, and the wood headboard lend an understated sophistication to the space.*

ABOVE: *This thoroughly contemporary bedroom possesses a peaceful tone, thanks to a balanced mixture of materials. Wooden built-in cabinetry offers a warm counterpoint to the cool metallic walls while maintaining the streamlined look of the space. This sleekness is also exhibited by the low platform bed—a modern interpretation of the Japanese futon—and the shoin-style screen, which allows natural light to enter while providing privacy.*

OPPOSITE: *A minimal use of furnishings, lamps with paper shades, and plenty of wood combine to give this bedroom an Asian overtone. The low-slung profile shared by the platform bed and night tables also contributes to the Eastern look.*

ABOVE: *Thanks to its color scheme, a modern chair sporting a vivid design mingles easily with the more traditional Eastern-style elements in this room. A large paper lantern and light from beyond the shoji screen illuminate the space.*

OPPOSITE: *This bedroom has a warm, natural feeling, thanks to an abundance of wood—used for the flooring, ceiling, walls, and built-in storage—and bamboo shades that gently filter sunlight. A display niche showcasing a celadon vase offers an interpretation of the traditional tokonoma.*

RIGHT: *Often made of cypress, the soaking tub is the key element in a Japanese bath. This one is positioned to give bathers the benefit of a refreshing garden view.*

LEFT: *Nestled into a windowed alcove, this tub promises to pamper the body and rejuvenate the soul. The wooded area outside is complemented indoors by a flagstone wall and a potted orchid, both of which heighten the natural environment.*

OPPOSITE: *This enticing bath is deftly integrated with the adjacent outdoor garden, thanks to the clever employment of earth-toned tiles. The use of these tiles on both the tub and the floor creates an organic look, as though the tub were flowing into the floor like water.*

ABOVE: *Engulfed by seamless expanses of glass, this tub creates the sensation of bathing outdoors. To enhance the Zen-like quality of the space, the bathing area is left virtually bare. The only accessories are ones that serve a clearly defined purpose.*

ABOVE: *Brick-shaped tiles and dark flooring combine to create a low-maintenance bath. The cool, sleek surfaces are softened by the wood door frame and the wood accents on the tub. Although somewhat spare, the room is inviting.*

A B O V E : *This airy bamboo tray has been filled with select bathing products. Black soaps, which evoke the smooth stones found in Japanese rock gardens, join with a white washcloth for a stylish but simple presentation.*

ABOVE: *Simplicity of form adds beauty to any space. Here, a gracefully curved chrome faucet, attached to a wooden soaking tub, lends elegance to a screen-enclosed bath. Notice the depth of the tub, which allows bathers to be submerged up to their shoulders. In the traditional ritual, the water is extremely hot.*

ABOVE: *Reminiscent of the black lacquer made from the sap of sumac trees native to southeast Asia, the surface of this above-the-counter basin brings a touch of exoticism to the setting. The shape of the sink calls to mind pottery made from slab construction, a technique often used by the Japanese for tableware. Notice the play of squares, which also appear in the black-and-white checkerboard pattern on the counter and the smooth block of soap. The angles and lines are softened, however, by a small leafy plant and a bamboo soap rest.*

RIGHT: *In this soothing setting, a continuous progression of monochromatic tiles establishes an appearance of fluidity. Wood blinds add warmth to the otherwise cool-toned milieu.*

PHOTOGRAPHY CREDITS

©J. Berman: 33

©Bjorg: 56 (designed by Tow Studios, styled by Wah), 68 (designed by Monica Chang, styled by Wah)

Corbis: 11, 17, 28, 43, 74, 75

©Richard Cummins: 31

Elizabeth Whiting Associates: 42, 85; ©Rodney Hyett: 14; ©Jerry Herpur: 34

©Michael Freeman: 21, 30, 44, 55, 58, 64, 87

©IMS Bildbyra: 92

©image/dennis krukowski: 25 (Robert Zion, Landscape Architect), 40 left (Geary Design), 80 (designed by Mazurca)

Interior Archive: ©Ken Hayden: 12, 36, 61, 70, 72, 91 (all designed by Jonathan Reed); ©Jonathan Pilkington: 7 (Owner: Max Rotheston), 79 (Owner: Max Rotheston); ©Fritz von der Schulenburg: 8, 41 (designed by Peter Hoffe/Serge Robin), 46, 76 (designed by Emily Todhunter), 84 (designed by Jed Johnson), 90 (designed by Peter Hoffe/Serge Robin); ©Edina van der Wyck: 49 left

©Jessie Walker Associates: 69, 93

©David Livingston: 89, 94

©Craig Lovell: 19, 20, 23, 26

©Ray Main/Mainstream: 13 (designed by Nick Allen), 38 (designed by Chris Cowper), 39 (designed by Chris Cowper), 59 (designed by Chris Cowper), 63 (designed by Plain and Simple Kitchens), 65, 95

©Joe Marvullo, Courtesy of Japan National Tourist Organization: 35

©Rob Melnychuk: 45 (designed by Fine Line Interiors), 82 (John Dow Medland, Architect)

©Michael Moran: 27 (designed by Tod Williams, Billie Tsien & Associates), 53 (designed by Tod Williams, Billie Tsien & Associates)

©Keith Scott Morton: 5, 32, 54

©Phillip Ennis Photography: 22 (Ferguson, Murray, Shamamian, Architects)

Courtesy of Roche Bobois: 71

©Eric Roth: 50 (designed by Michael Armsworthy)

©Brad Simmons Photography: 28–29

©David H. Smith: 18

©Tim Street-Porter: 62 (designed by Nicholai Septai),

©Brian Vanden Brink: 81

©Dominique Vorillon: 2, 40 right (designed by Tom Beeton/Tichenor & Thorp, Architects), 48, 49 right (designed by Brad Blair & Lotus Antiquities), 51 (designed by Brad Blair & Lotus Antiquities), 52 (designed by Brad Blair & Lotus Antiquities), 66 (designed by Tom Beeton/Tichenor & Thorp, Architects), 67 (designed by Tom Beeton/Tichenor & Thorp, Architects), 73 (designed by Tom Beeton/Tichenor & Thorp, Architects), 78 (designed by Kazuko Hoshino/William Hefner, Architect), 86 (designed by Foster Meagher, Architect), 88 (designed by Foster Meagher, Architect)

©Paul Warchol: 24, 47 (designed by Michael Strauss), 60 (designed by Studio Morsa), 83 (Robert Gurney, Architect)